ANXIETY JOURNAL

This journal was produced by Dayle Johnson & Tabitha Thompson
www.calmmindsclinic.com.au

Copyright (c) 2024 Calm Minds Clinic
All rights reserved.

ISBN: 978-1-7637459-0-2

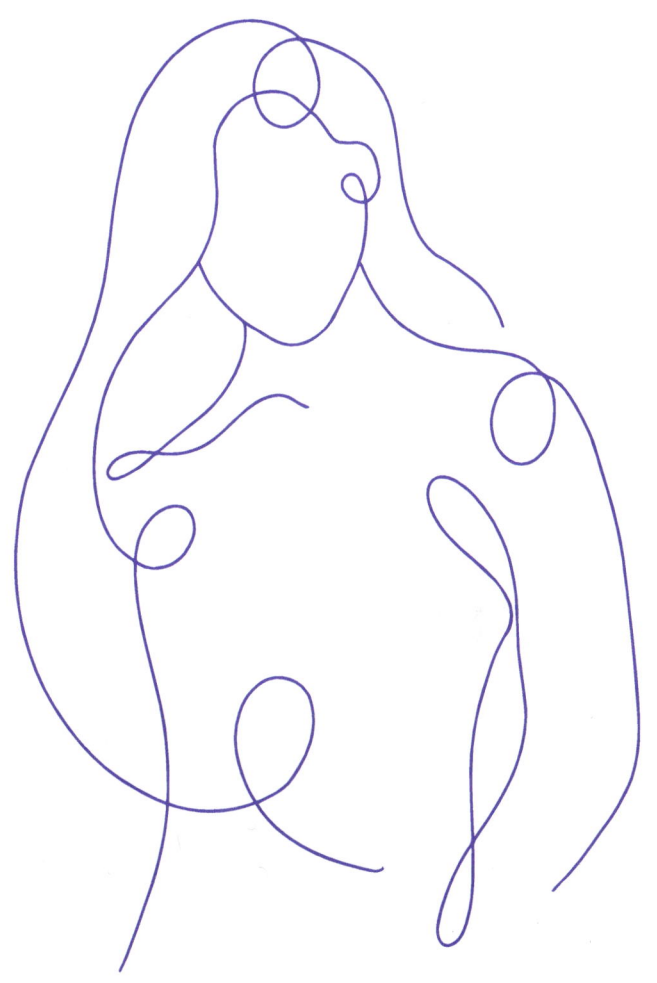

ABOUT YOU
(Yep, This Bit's All About You!)

Alright, let's get to know the star of this journal... let's keep it light, fun and as unique as you are!

Your Name (aka the legend holding this journal):

_____

Nickname (or what your mates call you):

_____

Three words that describe you (go ahead, brag a little!):

_____

Favourite place to chill out (real or imaginary):

_____

If your anxiety had a theme song, what would it be? 🎵

_____

What's something you're proud of, big or small?
(Go on, you deserve to feel proud!)

_____

That's it! Now, whenever you need a reminder of who's in control of this journey, just flip back to this page — because you're pretty amazing, and this journal is all about making sure you know that!

SELF-PORTRAIT

DRAW YOURSELF OR SOMETHING THAT REPRESENTS YOU HERE

WELCOME

Before we get started, how about we try something different?

Close your eyes for a moment (yes, right now) and take a big, deep breath.

In through your nose, notice the smell of the air around you...

Hold for a second and then slowly breathe out through your mouth.

Feel the air on your lips as you exhale, hear the sound it makes.

Feels good, doesn't it?

This journal is more than just pages of words; it's an experience. It's a place where you can let your thoughts wander, your pen dance and your senses come alive. Whether you're feeling a bit jittery or chilled out, this journal is here to help guide you through it all.

We've left heaps of space for you to scribble, draw or even just sit and feel the texture of the paper under your fingertips.

As you write, listen to the scratch of your pen or the rustle of the page. You might even catch a whiff of your favourite cuppa sitting nearby. Every little bit counts in helping you slow down, tune in and connect with your feelings.

So grab that pen, take a seat somewhere comfy, maybe even feel the warmth of the sun or a cool breeze — and let's make sense of anxiety in your own way.

You've got this, one page at a time!

Welcome to your personal anxiety journal!

This journal isn't just for writing down worries – it's here to help you understand and manage them. Think of it as a toolkit designed to guide you through those tough moments when anxiety feels a little too big to handle.

Created in collaboration with a registered Psychologist, it blends expert strategies with simple, practical exercises. Whether today's a good day, a challenging one or somewhere in between, this journal is here to help you make sense of it all and turn anxious moments into opportunities for growth.

Let's take this journey together!

PART 1
UNDERSTANDING ANXIETY

What is the Parasympathetic Nervous System?

Slows your heart rate and lowers blood pressure.

Helps your body relax and recover.

Saves energy and makes you feel calm.

Helps with things like sleep and feeling safe.

Helps with digestion by making your stomach and intestines work better.

Increases saliva to help with eating and digestion.

PART 1
UNDERSTANDING ANXIETY

In this first section, we explore what anxiety is and how it physiologically affects the body.

You'll learn about the body's natural stress responses – fight, flight, freeze and fawn and how they play a role in anxiety. Through this journal, we'll guide you in recognising these responses, understanding their impact and identifying ways to manage them. You'll also be introduced to practical tools like box breathing and body mapping, helping you calm your mind, reconnect with your body and take control of your anxiety.

Fight: The body's response to confront a perceived threat, preparing you to stand your ground or act aggressively to defend yourself.

Flight: The instinct to escape or avoid danger by fleeing from a stressful or threatening situation.

Freeze: A response where you feel 'frozen' or unable to act in the face of stress, often feeling stuck or paralysed.

Fawn: A reaction where you try to please or appease others to avoid conflict or danger, often by becoming overly compliant or submissive.

PART 1
UNDERSTANDING ANXIETY

ACTIVITY: Box Breathing (4-4-4-4)

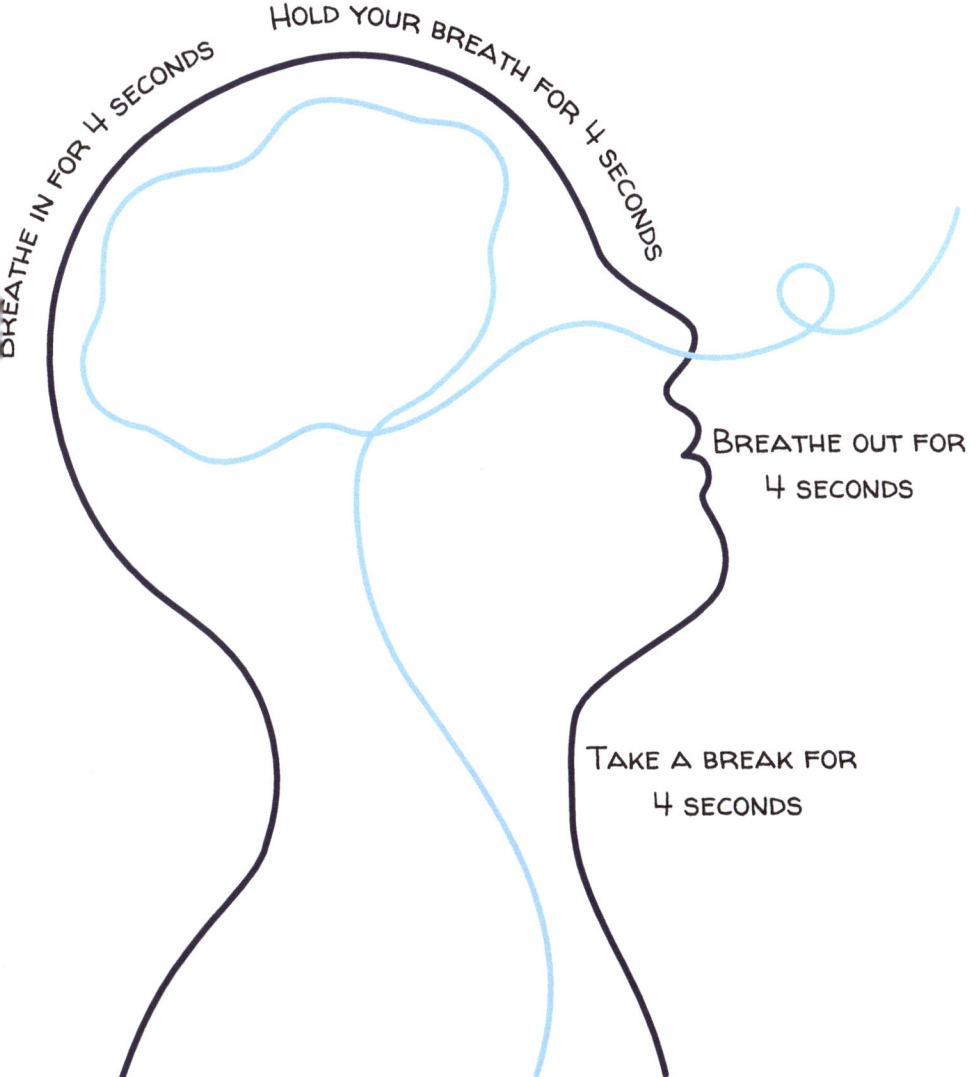

REPEAT THIS CYCLE TO HELP CALM YOUR MIND AND BODY.

PART 1
UNDERSTANDING ANXIETY

ACTIVITY: Body Map

Using a Body Map to track anxiety is like giving your body a voice! It helps you figure out where those sneaky feelings are hiding – whether it's knots in your stomach or a racing heart beat. Once you spot the tension, you can tackle it head-on. It's like having a personalised treasure map, but instead of finding gold, you're finding calm! The more you tune in, the easier it gets to handle those anxious vibes.

PART 1
UNDERSTANDING ANXIETY

ACTIVITY: Body Map

Tip! Mark down on the body map where you begin to notice your anxiety before it's at it's worst.

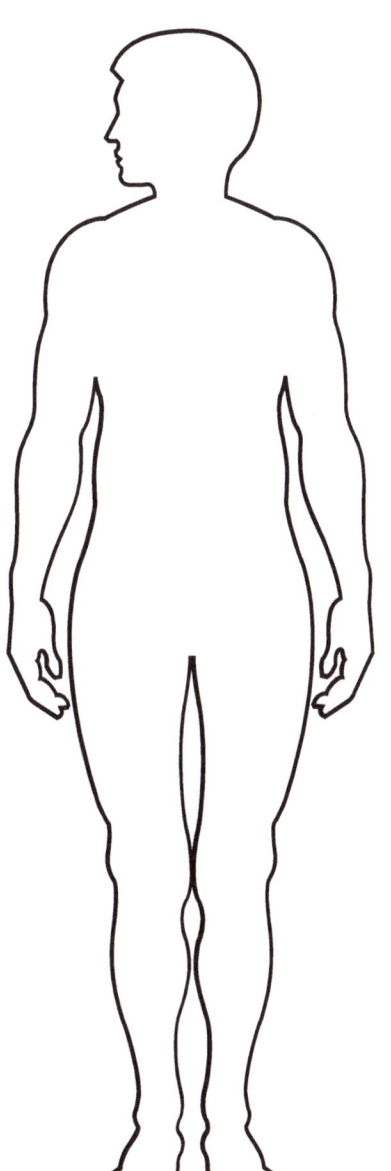

PART 1
A PLACE FOR YOUR NOTES

PART 2
GROUNDING TECHNIQUES

In this section, we'll dive into grounding techniques – practical methods to bring your mind back to the present and reduce anxiety. Grounding helps you reconnect with your surroundings and regain control when anxiety starts to take over. We've also included a fun, interactive quiz to help you 'Find Your Calm' and uncover personalised ways to manage your anxiety in different situations. These activities are designed to empower you with tools to stay calm and centered, no matter what life throws your way.

PART 2
GROUNDING TECHNIQUES

ACTIVITY: 5-4-3-2-1
Time to get grounded!

This simple exercise can help you hit pause and come back to the present moment. It's all about using your five senses to reconnect with what's happening right now. Ready to give it a go?

Find a comfy spot, take a slow, deep breath.

Look around and find 5 things you can see.
Take a moment to really notice what's around you. It could be anything — from the colour of the sky, a pattern on your socks or even the shape of your coffee cup. Write them down:
1.
2.
3.
4.
5.

Find 4 things you can feel.
What can you feel? Maybe the texture of your clothes, the softness of a cushion or the warmth of the sun beaming through your window.
1.
2.
3.
4.

PART 2
GROUNDING TECHNIQUES

ACTIVITY: 5-4-3-2-1
Time to get grounded!

Listen for 3 things you can hear.
Quiet your mind and focus on the sounds around you. There could be birds chirping, the hum of a fan or even your own breath.
1.
2.
3.

Name 2 things you can smell.
Take a deep breath and notice the scents in the air. Is it fresh rain, a candle or maybe just that hint of morning coffee?
1.
2.

Taste 1 thing.
If you've got something nearby, take a small bite or sip. If not, think about a recent taste you enjoyed — sweet fruit, the sandwich you had for lunch or even a bite of your favourite chocolate.
1.

And there you have it! The 5-4-3-2-1 technique is like a little mental reset button. Whenever things feel overwhelming, just come back to this page, and use your senses to ground yourself in the moment. You've got this!

PART 2
GROUNDING TECHNIQUES

ACTIVITY: 'Find your Calm' Quiz

Grab a pen and let's see what resonates with you.

1. When you feel anxious, what's your immediate instinct?
a) Take a deep breath and count to ten.
b) Go for a walk and soak up some nature.
c) Write down your thoughts or draw a picture.
d) Listen to music or a podcast.

2. Which of these sounds do you find calming?
a) The gentle rustle of leaves in the wind.
b) Soft instrumental music.
c) Waves crashing on the shore.
d) A warm, friendly voice reading a story.

3. If you had to choose a sensory item to carry with you, what would it be?
a) A small stress ball or fidget toy.
b) Scented essential oil.
c) A beautiful rock or crystal.
d) A comfy blanket or scarf.

PART 2
GROUNDING TECHNIQUES

ACTIVITY: 'Find your Calm' Quiz

4. When feeling overwhelmed, how do you prefer to express yourself?
a) Talking it out with a friend.
b) Writing your feelings down.
c) Creating art or crafts.
d) Moving my body – dancing or exercising!

5. What's your favourite way to connect with nature?
a) Strolling through a park or garden.
b) Sitting quietly by a river or beach.
c) Gardening or tending to plants.
d) Taking a hike in the bush or mountains.

6. How do you prefer to unwind after a long day?
a) Meditating or practicing yoga.
b) Enjoying a warm bath with candles.
c) Curling up with a good book or movie.
d) Cooking or baking something yummy!

PART 2
GROUNDING TECHNIQUES

ACTIVITY: 'Find your Calm' Quiz

7. WHICH OF THESE QUOTES RESONATE WITH YOU?
A) "I CAN GET THROUGH THIS."
B) "I AM HERE. I AM SAFE."
C) "BREATHE IN, BREATHE OUT."
D) "I AM IN CONTROL OF MY THOUGHTS."

TALLY YOUR ANSWERS!
COUNT HOW MANY TIMES YOU SELECTED EACH LETTER:
- A): _____
- B): _____
- C): _____
- D): _____

PART 2
GROUNDING TECHNIQUES

ACTIVITY: 'Find your Calm' Quiz

RESULTS:

- MOSTLY A'S: THE MINDFUL BREATHER
- YOU FIND CALM THROUGH BREATHING TECHNIQUES AND MINDFULNESS PRACTICES. KEEP A LIST OF DEEP BREATHING EXERCISES HANDY!

- MOSTLY B'S: THE NATURE LOVER
- NATURE IS YOUR GO-TO GROUNDING SOURCE! PLAN REGULAR WALKS OR OUTDOOR ACTIVITIES TO RECONNECT WITH THE NATURAL WORLD.

- MOSTLY C'S: THE CREATIVE SOUL
- EXPRESSING YOURSELF THROUGH ART AND WRITING HELPS GROUND YOU. SET ASIDE TIME FOR CREATIVITY IN YOUR DAILY ROUTINE.

- MOSTLY D'S: THE ACTIVE MOVER
- MOVEMENT IS YOUR GROUNDING FORCE! INCORPORATE EXERCISE OR DANCE INTO YOUR DAY TO SHAKE OFF ANXIETY AND BOOST YOUR MOOD.

REMEMBER:

EVERYONE'S JOURNEY IS UNIQUE! TAKE A MOMENT TO REFLECT ON YOUR RESULTS AND CONSIDER TRYING OUT DIFFERENT GROUNDING TECHNIQUES THAT RESONATE WITH YOU. EMBRACE THE ONES THAT MAKE YOU FEEL CALM.

PART 2
A PLACE FOR YOUR NOTES

PART 3
RESILIENCE BUILDING

This section is all about strengthening your resilience — the ability to bounce back and adapt, even when anxiety feels overwhelming. Resilience doesn't mean never feeling anxious; it's about learning how to manage it and keep moving forward. Through habit tracking and reflective journal prompts, you'll discover patterns, build healthy coping strategies and develop the mental capability to face challenges with confidence.

These strategies can help you be more resilient and prepared to handle stress and anxiety.

PART 3
RESILIENCE BUILDING

ACTIVITY: Habit Tracker

This habit tracker is all about you — your routines, your achievements and your unique journey to a calmer, more centred self. Each habit you track is like adding a stepping stone along your path. The more you lay down, the better things become.

Create Your Path: Draw or print a grid for the month (or use a calendar). On the side, list the habits you want to track. Leave space to tick off or colour in each day you complete them. Each habit gets you closer to building your unique, balanced life.

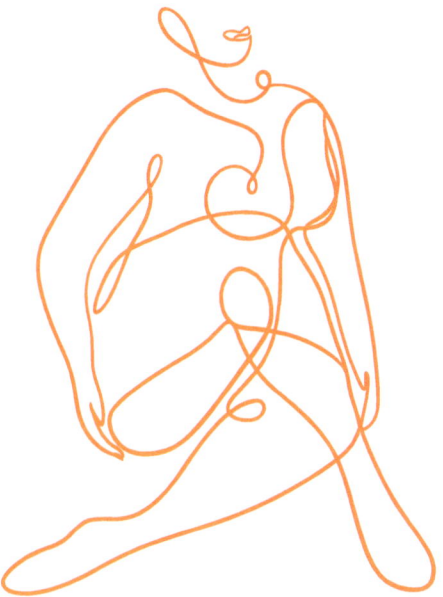

PART 3
RESILIENCE BUILDING

ACTIVITY: Habit Tracker

Choose Your Habits: Select up to 5 habits that you want to build consistency around. These could be habits that nourish your body or your mind. For example:

- Drink 2 litres of water
- Move your body for 20 minutes
- Spend 10 minutes meditating or practising mindfulness
- Spend time writing in your journal each day
- Go to bed by 10 PM

You can also include fun habits, like 'Take a deep breath and enjoy the moment' or 'Spend 5 minutes in nature. Feel the soles of your feet on the green grass'.

Track Your Progress: Every day you complete a habit, mark it on your tracker. You could use a simple tick, colour in the box or use a different symbol. Each habit you track represents one more step forward in your personal journey.

Reflect and Celebrate Milestones: At the end of each week, take a moment to reflect on your progress. Did you practice all your habits? What worked well and where could you improve? Use this reflection to stay mindful of your journey and celebrate the small wins – consistency is key!

PART 3
RESILIENCE BUILDING

ACTIVITY: Habit Tracker

ERSONAL REWARDS: THINK OF SIMPLE THINGS THAT BRING YOU JOY. HESE ARE YOUR REWARDS FOR STAYING ON TRACK — FROM SMALL ELF-CARE TREATS TO EXPERIENCES YOU LOVE. IT'S IMPORTANT TO CKNOWLEDGE YOUR PROGRESS.

Reflections and Adjustments: Life is ever-changing. Some weeks you'll nail all your habits and other weeks might need some adjustments. That's part of the journey! Write a few notes in your reflection section to guide you along the way.

QUARTERLY CHECK-IN: EVERY THREE MONTHS, REVIEW YOUR HABITS. ASK YOURSELF: ARE THESE HABITS STILL IMPORTANT TO ME? WOULD I LIKE TO ADD OR CHANGE ANY? THIS GIVES YOU FLEXIBILITY AND CONTROL OVER YOUR PERSONAL GROWTH.

Tracking habits can keep the focus on you and your individual progress. Instead of competing or achieving external goals, you're creating space for personal eflection, growth and balance. By tracking your habits and celebrating small milestones, you build a sense of chievement and keep moving forward in your journey. It's flexible, personal and grounded in mindfulness — all while being fun and motivational.

HABIT TRACKER

MORNING HABITS	M	T	W	T	F	S	S
	○	○	○	○	○	○	○
	○	○	○	○	○	○	○
	○	○	○	○	○	○	○
	○	○	○	○	○	○	○
	○	○	○	○	○	○	○

AFTERNOON HABITS	M	T	W	T	F	S	S
	○	○	○	○	○	○	○
	○	○	○	○	○	○	○
	○	○	○	○	○	○	○
	○	○	○	○	○	○	○

NIGHT ROUTINE	M	T	W	T	F	S	S
	○	○	○	○	○	○	○
	○	○	○	○	○	○	○
	○	○	○	○	○	○	○
	○	○	○	○	○	○	○
	○	○	○	○	○	○	○

HABIT REFLECTIONS

Reflecting on your habit tracking is essential for understanding your progress and celebrating your wins! It helps you see what's working, spot patterns and adjust your goals as needed. This process boosts motivation and keeps you mindful of your emotions, making it easier to create a balanced routine that supports your wellbeing. So, take a moment to pause, reflect and appreciate how far you've come!

WHAT WORKED

WHAT DIDN'T WORK

PART 3
A PLACE FOR YOUR NOTES

PART 3
RESILIENCE BUILDING

ACTIVITY: Reflective Journal Prompts

My greatest strengths are...

I use my greatest strengths when I'm...

I'm proud of myself when I...

Recognising your strengths boosts self-confidence and resilience, making it easier to tackle challenges and achieve your goals.

PART 3
RESILIENCE BUILDING

ACTIVITY: Reflective Journal Prompts

I BELIEVE IN MYSELF BECAUSE I'M...

I FEEL CONFIDENT WHEN I'M...

I FEEL CALM WHEN...

Discovering what makes you feel calm is about identifying the activities, thoughts or practices that bring you peace and help you regain control when anxiety arises.

PART 3
RESILIENCE BUILDING

ACTIVITY: Reflective Journal Prompts

I WILL...

PROGRESS LOOKS LIKE...

SUCCESS MEANS...

Overcoming anxiety means acknowledging its presence, identifying triggers and using coping strategies to regain control, ultimately leading to a greater sense of peace and confidence.

PART 3

A PLACE FOR YOUR NOTES

PART 4
ANXIETY ACTION PLAN

In this final section, you'll create your personalised Anxiety Action Plan — a guide to managing anxiety when it strikes. This plan can help you recognise early signs of anxiety, implement coping strategies quickly and outline specific actions to regain control in stressful moments.

Whether it's breathing techniques, grounding exercises or reaching out for support, your action plan can be your go-to resource for calming your mind and navigating through anxious situations with clarity and confidence.

PART 4
ANXIETY ACTION PLAN

My Anxiety triggers and symptoms are...

My go-to grounding techniques are...

The people I can reach out to for support are...

Space to Sketch my Thoughts...

Today's Adventure in my Head

Scribbles of my Day

Brain Full. Time to Spill...

Finding Calm in Chaos...

The Great Anxiety Escape

Brain Break

Conquering Fears

My Mind on Paper...

Planting Seeds

Drawing my way to Calm...

Today's Forecast:
100% Chance of Randomness

A Creative Escape

Plot Twist:
I forgot what I was thinking!

When Words Fail...

Embracing the Here and Now

Mindful Moments on Paper...

Brain Shenanigans: Expect the Unexpected!

When Emotions get Abstract...

Taming the Anxiety Dragon

Scribbling my Emotions

My Daily Dose of Positive Thoughts

When Colours and Feelings Collide...

Chasing Dreams, Not Worries

My Masterpiece of Mindfulness

Adventures in Overthinking

Sketching my Inner World

Welcome to the Circus of my Thoughts

A Place to be Me

Where Moonlight meets my Musings

Silence my Worries

Curiosity and Chaos: A Day in My Head

Art is my Safe Space...

Diary of a Reformed Worrier

It's a 'Drawing my Thoughts' Kind of Day

Today's Adventures brought to you by my Brain

Finding Calm through Creativity

My Worry-Free Zone

When Lines Speak Louder than Words

My Journey to Joy

Set me Free...

www.ingramcontent.com/pod-product-compliance
Lightning Source LLC
Chambersburg PA
CBHW041808160426
43209CB00016B/1724